Heads Up!

How To Use This Book

There are lots of extras in this book aimed at helping you with writing your essay.

BRAIN JAM

Brain Jams offer activities to get you thinking creatively and give you a chance to hone your skills.

★ PROJECT JUMP START

Project Jump Starts provide that sometimes necessary extra push to get you going on your own essay.

TIP FILE

Tip Files offer up all sorts of helpful suggestions and hints on getting the project done.

RESOURCES   RESOURCES

One of these icons will lead you to more information.

ORDINARY   EXTRAORDINARY

Throughout the book you will see the ordinary and the extraordinary side by side. With revisions and some thought, these comparisons show you what you can accomplish.

Photographs © 2005: Corbis Images/Bettmann: 10, 54.

Cover design: Marie O'Neill
Page design: Simon Says Design!
Cover and interior illustrations by Kevin Pope.

Library of Congress Cataloging-in-Publication Data

Orr, Tamra.
  Extraordinary essays / by Tamra Orr.
      p. cm. — (F. W. Prep)
  Includes bibliographical references and index.
  ISBN 0-531-16761-5 (lib. bdg.)   0-531-17576-6 (pbk.)
  1. Essay—Authorship. I. Title. II. Series.
  PN4500.O77 2005
  808.4—dc22
                                              2005007299

EXTRAORDINARY
Essays

by Tamra Orr

Franklin Watts®

A Division of Scholastic Inc.
New York • Toronto • London • Auckland • Sydney
Mexico City • New Delhi • Hong Kong.
• Danbury, Connecticut

EXTRAORDINARY ESSAYS

ASSIGNMENT:

You've got yet another essay to write for English class, science class, or history class. Sometimes it may seem that you're lost in a sea of essays (all of them due at roughly the same time, of course). By the time you finish high school, you'll probably have a drawer full of graded essays.

Why so many? Essays are a part of the plan your state has for your education. Each state in the country has its own educational curriculum plan for you and other students in your state. These plans are called educational standards. From **Oregon** to **Maine**, from **Minnesota** to **Texas**, the standards call for students to tackle a variety of essay projects. In **Oregon**, for instance, eighth graders are expected to write persuasive compositions that include a well-defined thesis. **Florida** wants students in grades nine through twelve to be able to draft and revise writing that is focused and purposeful.

ESSAY

So see, you're not alone. Thousands of other students are tackling descriptive essays, persuasive essays, and many other types of essays this year. That means like you, they're hitting the books, searching library shelves, and surfing the Internet. They are outlining, writing, and revising their ideas. So how do you give your essay a twist that makes it distinct from all the others? In a word, how do you make it EXTRAORDINARY?

Part of making any project EXTRAORDINARY —whether it's a short story, essay, or research project—is knowing what is expected of you and surpassing those expectations. Regard expectations as opportunities for you to develop and express your own creative ideas while developing your skills as a writer and storyteller. Writing essays is also useful preparation for your future. Expressing your ideas clearly in words or on paper will make you shine in any job.

Today's essay forecast calls for well-defined theses in the Pacific Northwest . . . And those in the Southeast can expect a flood of drafts and revisions . . .

Check Out Your State's Standards!

One way to stay ahead of the game is to take a look at your state's standards for this year and the years ahead. If you're ready to look into your future, try visiting the Developing Educational Standards site at:
http://www.edstandards.org/Standards.html

On it, you can find links to the educational departments of every state and even focus on language arts in particular. For more of a national overview of language arts standards, let's take a look at a few of the twelve national educational standards created by the National Council of Teachers of English (NCTE). (For a complete list, visit NCTE's Web site, **http://www.ncte.org.**)

By researching and writing extraordinary essays, you demonstrate several key skills mentioned in the standards:

- An extraordinary essay indicates that you know how to use written language to communicate effectively with a range of audiences and for different purposes.

- The creative and logical tools you use while writing an extraordinary essay demonstrates your knowledge of writing strategies and the writing process and your ability to use them effectively.

- An extraordinary essay is an example of your knowledge of language structure, language conventions, figurative language, and genre and shows that you can employ this knowledge to create texts.

- An extraordinary essay involves conducting research, posing questions, and probing problems on a topic.

- To create an extraordinary essay you must gather and analyze information from a variety of sources, including technological resources.

Heads Up!

So Here's the Scoop

When teachers grade essays, they use a number of factors to determine your score. This information will change from class to class and teacher to teacher, but these are the general guidelines for how your essay will be graded:

Focus. Is it clear?

Evidence. Were there enough supporting facts, examples, or statistics?

Structure. Is the information presented in a logical order?

Grammar. Are there any grammar errors?

Punctuation. Is the paper punctuated properly?

Spelling. Are there any misspelled words in the paper?

Word usage. Did you use lively verbs and strong vocabulary words?

What's an Essay Anyway?

It is little surprise that the word "essay" comes from the French word for "try." When you are writing an essay, you are trying to convey or share a message, image, thought, or process through your words. If you don't choose the right words, follow the right format, or stick to the right structure, your essay will not achieve its goal.

Writing essays in school is important. That is made obvious by the number of them that are assigned. But an essay is more than just five paragraphs. It is an organized piece of writing that has a central thesis with details and support.

Writing essays is often required when you pursue a college education as well. It is common to find them on college and scholarship applications. What you write will make your application stand out far more than having a 3.45 GPA instead of a 3.24. Universities want students who can get their points across, who can articulate their thoughts, and who can answer the questions they are asked. Having the skill to write a strong essay will do that. Of course, those abilities will come in quite handy in those required English classes, too!

"A good essay must have this permanent quality about it; it must draw its curtain round us, but it must be a curtain that shuts us in, not out."
—Virginia Woolf (1882–1941)

Even beyond college, you may find yourself writing essays or something similar on the job. They are very important to the rest of your life, too. If you think your last essay is written just before you grab your diploma, think again. There will be more opportunities in the future to write essays—and sometimes, doing it well can make a real difference.

For example, let's say you and a zillion other people are applying for a great new job. When you get to the last question on the job application, and the employer asks something like "Explain why you are the kind of person who would benefit our company" or "What experience have you had that has most affected your outlook on life?" you will know what to do. You will not be one of the other applicants, who are looking panic-stricken and slightly nauseated. Instead, you will have the skill to write an essay that may just get that potential boss to sit up and take notice.

Many jobs require writing skills, whether it is for sharing meeting notes with others, or as part of the promotion process or for communicating with staff and/or customers. Writing skills are essential to have long after you receive your high-school diploma.

There are a number of different essay types, but here are the primary ones you will learn about in this book:

Descriptive

The descriptive essay focuses on a person, place, or thing. One of the keys to handling this type of essay is to use language to invoke the five senses so that readers feel as if they are seeing through your eyes and sharing your experience.

Process

The process essay shows the steps involved in a project, concept, or event. It can be as simple as how to plant a seed and as complex as how acid rain damages crops. No matter what subject you must tackle, think of it as your opportunity to show someone how to do something or how something works.

Compare and Contrast

The compare and contrast essay involves two or more things and explores the similarities and differences between them. In your essay, you want to answer these questions: How are things the same? How are they different?

Persuasive

The persuasive essay is driven by a strong argument that is well supported by evidence. Even though it is sometimes called "argumentative," this type of essay allows you to convince, inform, and enlighten your readers, not force them to accept your viewpoint.

Book Reports/Personal Narratives

A book report is a type of essay often assigned in English class with the goal of showing that you've read the book, understand its major themes, and have a well-articulated point of view of the work. A personal narrative is a chance to share an experience of yours in the form of an essay. These commonly requested types of writing can be fun and unique, once you start looking at them from new angles.

SAT Essay

Taking the Scholastic Aptitude Test (SAT) involves writing an essay in response to a writing prompt. The essay component of the test has a time limit of 25 minutes. This is an essay that requires clarity, accuracy, and speed.

So What's an Essay?

An essay is:

A relatively short prose composition.

Focused on one subject.

Usually personal in nature.

Most essays consist of:

A topic

A thesis

Supporting evidence

play word ga

ok at Photo alb

Scan Indexes

what grabs your inte

Surf the
internet

HUNT AND GATHER

Finding Your Idea

Finding Your Idea

All great essays begin with the very same thing: an outstanding idea. Fortunately, ideas are limitless, even if you've been assigned a topic. There's a reason why most assigned topics are very broad; general topics give you lots of room to find an idea that grabs your interest.

Ideas can come from inside, but there are a lot of outside sources that help you tap into them. As you figure out which idea is best for you, keep these things in mind:

First look at your assignment. Are there any instructions on what topic to cover? Some assignments can be very specific, such as the role of child labor during the Industrial Revolution, while others can be more open-ended, like compare and contrast your favorite type of music, rap, with your least favorite, classical. Read the assignment at least twice to make sure you know all of the details. You don't want to waste your time pursuing ideas that could be absolutely fascinating, but completely wrong for the assignment.

TIP FILE

Try paraphrasing the assignment for yourself. Writing down the focus, objectives, and restrictions for your essay in your own words is a great way to start developing your own take on the project.

Assignment Checklist

The very best source of information about your essay is your teacher and the assignment he or she gave you. Before you begin looking for an idea, look at what details the assignment already told you:

- **Topic.** Did the teacher already suggest a topic or focus?

- **Type.** What kind of essay is it supposed to be? Persuasive? Descriptive? Process?

- **Required information.** Did your teacher tell you of certain facts, opinions, references, material, or anything else that you are to include in the essay?

- **Word length.** How long should it be?

- **Format.** Does it have to be typed? Double-spaced?

- **Due date.** When does it have to be done?

If possible, choose an idea that fits your interests, knowledge, and background. If the assignment is to write about a sport, for example, pick one that you play or watch—or at least would like to if given the chance. If you choose a topic that you care about personally, the research and the writing will be easier and more fun.

Get a Box!

As you find images, articles, and other material for your essay, you may want to get a box or a binder to hold your possible inspirations. This way, once you're done hunting and gathering, you can easily review what you've got. Newspaper and magazine articles, advertisements, quotes, favorite books, and historical facts are all potential sparks for your great essay. An extraordinary idea could come from anywhere.

Creating a Brainstorm!

When it comes to finding great ideas, your own brain is one of the best places to start. Get out a piece of paper and one of your favorite pens or pencils. Now, without worrying about grammar, spelling, punctuation, or even the relevance of the idea, start mapping out ideas related to the topic. Your ideas can be in the form of words or phrases.

For example, you've got to write about an endangered species. Write the words "endangered species" in the center of your paper and start writing anything and everything you can think of related to that phrase: Siberian tigers, hunting, whaling, fur, habitat, oil spills, accidents, alligators, and so on.

Once you feel like your brain is completely drained of all possibilities, look at your paper. Take the time to explore each idea written on it. Eliminate the ones you know are great but will not fit the assignment, and focus on the ones that have potential.

Be ruthless. Narrow down your ideas by asking yourself, "Does this fit what the teacher assigned? Is it focused enough? Is it interesting?" At this stage, the idea may still be too general, but it will give you a place to start.

Searching for Ideas in All the
Right Places

Do you think that there just aren't sources of inspiration within a ten-mile radius? Here is a list of some of the best places to look, and most are within a few feet:

- **Look in the newspaper** for local, state, and national stories.

- **Check out the magazines** you and your family have around the house.

- **Read your journal** and see if you mentioned anything that could become an essay topic.

- **Grab a photo album** and see what thoughts it inspires.

- **See what is on your bookshelf:** titles, chapter names, and subject matter can trigger an idea.

- **Page through** your class textbooks for possibilities.

- **Surf the net** for news stories, debates related to your topic, and cutting-edge research questions.

- **Call your friends** and see what topics come up that might work in an essay.

- **Listen to the dinner conversation** of your family, and watch out for ideas.

- **Watch a movie** or television show and see what ideas occur to you.

- **Play word games,** such as Mad Libs®, Scrabble®, or word jumbles.

- **Attend a local town or association meeting** to hear what issues are being discussed.

- **View the advertising** you see around you with a critical eye.

EXTRA HELP

Let others do some of the hard work for you. If you are still stumped for an idea, check out these titles:

- *The Pocket Muse: Ideas and Inspiration for Writing* by Monica Wood (Writer's Digest Books, 2002).

- *The Writer's Block: 786 Ideas to Jump-Start Your Imagination* by Jason Rekulak (Running Press Books, 2001).

- *What Can I Write About? 7,000 Topics for High School Students* by David Powell (National Council of Teachers of English, 2002).

- *10,000 Ideas for Term Papers, Projects, Reports and Speeches: Intriguing, Original Research Topics for Every Student's Needs* by Kathryn Lamm (Arco Publishing, 1998).

About my essay . . .

From Good to Great: Giving Your Topic the Right Spin

Before you decide on the right spin, you have to make sure your idea is the right size. Ask yourself a question: Is your topic big enough to be an entire book? If so, it is probably too broad. For example, if you have been assigned to write an essay about something that relates to the weather, the topic of natural catastrophes would be too broad. Even if you narrowed it down to tornadoes, it would be too broad.

Don't go too far in the other direction, though, and narrow it down to the wind speed of one single tornado. Instead, pick one example of a weather-related disaster, and discuss its highlights.

Once you have an idea of the right size, it is time to focus on, well, focus. This is the slant, angle, or "spin" you will put on your idea. It's the way to make a usual idea unusual.

TIP FILE

Keep a pad of paper near your bed. You never know when you might be inspired. Your idea may come to you in the middle of the night, just as you are drifting off, or during those first few moments of being awake in the morning.

Let's look at a few examples.

Let's say you are supposed to write an essay for history class. How about the Wright brothers and their role in the history of flight? You could write on "How the Wright Brothers Revolutionized Flight." That might be a good essay. A little extra research and thought, however, might lead you in another direction altogether. You could write on "The Lesson of Failure." The Wright brothers didn't just build a plane and fly; they built lots of them that didn't fly and lots that crashed first. You could focus on "The Other Wright: Orville and Wilbur's Sister." Katharine was very influential in her brothers' invention and how it developed.

How about an essay for science class? You have been assigned to write something from the unit you just finished on the future of reproduction. You could write "A Look at Reproduction in the Future." On the other hand, you could write "Creating Designer Babies: The World of Genetic Choices" or even "Multiple Mess: The Possibility of Being Cloned." Which would you rather read?

Maybe you have been asked to write the story of your life. Your idea could be "My Life So Far." It is accurate, but a bit dull. How about "A Modern-Day Red Riding Hood: Life Living with My Grandmother" or "The Life of a Superstar: Part One"?

LOOKING FOR CONTROVERSY?

If you're looking for a controversial topic for your essay, ElectraGuide **http://www.ozline.com/electraguide/** has a few suggestions for you. You can scroll fifty suggested topics and even use the Thesis Builder tool to get you started.

Find a Different Perspective

Taking your idea from ordinary to extraordinary is the process of looking at your idea from all sides and finding the unusual angle. It's there. As a sign in my office says, **"Startle yourself: Look at an idea upside down."**

Here are several ways to do this:

- **Take the textbook from the class the essay is for and turn to the index.** Scan topics and listings. Is there something interesting there? A new idea? An intriguing subject? Follow it up.

- **If you are writing about a person, look at his or her life from a different angle.** What might his or her parents have said about this person? What might a neighbor have thought? What would you have thought if he or she was your best friend?

- **If you are writing about an event, think of the minor characters who might have been involved.** Instead of writing about the generals who strategized during a war, write about the boy whose job it was to feed and water the soldiers' horses or the girl who delivered bandages to the wounded.

- **If you are writing about a place, how would you describe it from the viewpoint of an animal?** An alien? An old man? A young child?

Some authors have written entire books using these ideas. A number of authors have written about the Lewis and Clark expedition from the viewpoint of Clark's dog, Seaman. Gregory Maguire has rewritten some famous stories in his novels. In *Wicked*, he imagines the life story of the Wicked Witch of the West from *The Wizard of Oz*. By taking a look at a lesser-known character from a very famous story, Maguire was able to create a fantastical story of his own.

So What's Your Point?

Let's look at a few typical thesis statements and see how they could be improved.

ORDINARY	EXTRAORDINARY
I am going to write about a terrific television show that everyone knows.	Is there anyone under the age of twenty-one who doesn't know who Rachel, Monica, Phoebe, Ross, Chandler, and Joey are?

Starting an essay with a question often draws readers in quickly. Starting with "I am going to write about" is one of the best ways to put them to sleep.

ORDINARY	EXTRAORDINARY
Vampire stories have been around for more than a century.	The image of mysterious men sucking the lifeblood from desperate damsels in distress has haunted literature for more than one hundred years.

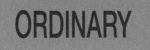

By adding vivid vocabulary and setting the scene, the reader will want to read on.

ORDINARY	EXTRAORDINARY
This essay will tell you how to change a flat tire in three simple steps.	There is little worse than getting caught out in a cold rain, without an umbrella, and with an auto emergency. Here is how to avoid that in three simple steps.

You have involved the reader immediately and given him or her a reason to keep going.

Once you have found your idea, it is time to gather the information you need to support it. Some of that research may simply be sitting down and remembering or asking your parents or friends for some details. A lot of research will require the Internet, a library, and other sources. Now it's time to try and prove your point.

BRAIN JAM:
Tackling Topics, Creating a Thesis

Get a good fit. Once you have your topic, you've got to narrow the focus to make it manageable. Take a piece of paper and write the general topic at the top. Develop two or more different subtopics and write them down below the general topic. Continue drilling the different strands down as far as possible. The beginnings of each strand are probably too general, and the endings of each strand are probably too specific. Review the middle of each strand to see which topic grabs your interest.

Craft a thesis. A great thesis statement is a work of art, and it requires some effort to come up with an extraordinary one. See how many variations you can come up with using the two basic ingredients in a thesis: a topic and an assertion.

Identify your question. Revise your thesis statement so it reads as a question. With your main question in hand, develop three questions that would lead up to the answer to your main question.

FRANKLIN
CHAPTER 2
WATTS

THE VISION

Prove Your Thesis

Prove Your Thesis

Now it's time to do the research to back up your extraordinary idea. How much research you have to do depends greatly on two things:

 what type of essay you are writing, and

 how much you already know about the topic.

For example, if you've been asked to write an autobiographical essay, you are the best resource. Who knows more about you than you? You will likely have to ask your family for some help with the details, of course. On the other hand, if you have been asked to write about the history of the postal system, you are most likely going to spend hours conducting research. How and where you do that research can certainly affect your essay and its grade.

Notes on Notes

Before helping you find your crucial pieces of information, we need to talk about how you're going to collect and organize all of this essential stuff. While they may seem old-fashioned, note cards (also known as index cards) are cheap, easy, and effective tools. There's a reason why, in these digital times, you still find people using them. Consider getting the ones that are bound in a spiral notebook so you won't lose or drop one or forget the order in which they go.

If you've ever gone to a restaurant and gotten a waiter who doesn't write down your order but says he will remember it, you know there's a high risk that you will get the wrong food. When it comes to researching a paper, don't fool yourself into thinking you will remember everything you read. You have to take notes on your sources if you want to make sure you get the facts right.

Write Down Major Points

As you read your research material (book, article, Web site, etc.), **write down the major points or highlights as you do when you are taking notes in class.** How you organize the notes will depend somewhat on the kind of essay you are writing, but put some kind of title on each note card to guide you later. If you are working on that essay about cybercrime, for instance, you could label cards "Crime statistics," "Interview with Mr. Connors, computer security expert," "Info on privacy organizations," etc. This way, when you are writing your paper, you can easily find the notes you need for each section of it. You don't have to write things down word for word (unless you think the material might make a great direct quote). Instead you can summarize the source material. You might want to create your own shorthand so it goes more quickly. Just make sure you can figure it out later. A good way to make writing faster is to use abbreviations for common words.

Citations and References

If you are going to quote someone directly or cite a statistic, always include the title of the resource and the page number on which you found the information so you know exactly where it came from. Be sure to keep a separate list of the resources you use to create your bibliography, or works cited list. For example, if you were writing a persuasive paper about the possible risks of chronic dieting, one of your note cards might look like this:

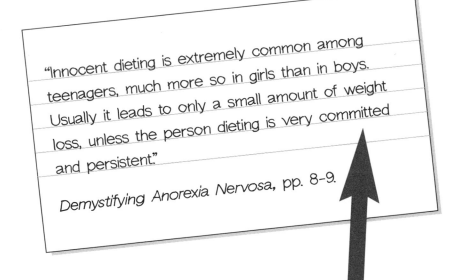

"Innocent dieting is extremely common among teenagers, much more so in girls than in boys. Usually it leads to only a small amount of weight loss, unless the person dieting is very committed and persistent."

Demystifying Anorexia Nervosa, pp. 8–9.

The card above shows a direct quotation.
Quotes from experts can be a powerful way to support your thesis.

When you decide to use a direct quotation, make sure to double-check that you got all of the words right and in the right order.

There are slight differences in style for each type of source, but here is a quick look at the most common ones:

- **BOOK:** Lucas, M.D., Alexander. *Demystifying Anorexia Nervosa.* New York: Oxford University Press, 2004.

- **MAGAZINE:** Lawler, Brian P. "To Help Other People," *Boy's Life,* March 2004: 34–39.

- **INTERNET SITE:** CNN.com 2005. CNN Network. January 9, 2005. <http://www.cnn.com>

For more information, you might want to check the *Modern Language Association's MLA Handbook for Writers of Research Papers* for more information on formatting.

Go to the Source

There are three main ways to conduct research in today's world. The first is by reading published information, which can be divided into primary and secondary sources. A primary source is one that comes directly from an eyewitness to an event. It can be a diary, journal, story, article, or speech. If you were doing a report on the atom bomb, for example, and you used information from a newspaper article written by a journalist who actually saw the blast, that would be a primary source. If you read a book about the atom bomb by a person who had studied about it, that would be a secondary source. Obviously, a primary source is more authentic. Quotes from these sources can be exciting and give your report a truly "YOU . . . are THERE!" feeling. There's a reason teachers often ask that you use primary sources in your work.

Start at the Library

Good sources of published information are books, magazines, newspapers, encyclopedias, dictionaries, and textbooks. A trip to a library will help you in your search because you're likely to find all of these different types of sources there. If your local library doesn't have a source you want, it may be able to get it for you through interlibrary loan. If there is a college or university nearby, see if you can visit its library. College libraries tend to have very large collections of books, periodicals, and other informational resources.

If you are going to write a paper on alcoholism, for example, start at a library. Keep your focus in mind as you look for information. What aspect of this disease will you be emphasizing? If you're writing about the effect of alcohol on the brain, you need a medical reference book that gives you that information. If you are writing about teen binge drinking, look at newspapers and magazines that can give you up-to-date stories and statistics. A video can show you biological processes and first-person accounts of people coping with this problem.

Finding Good Articles

A good way to find magazine articles on your subject is to look through such resources as *The Reader's Guide to Periodical Literature.* It lists topics in alphabetical order and then, by year, shows what magazines have published articles on that topic and where to find them.

Other sources include a publication's main Web site and online databases and online card catalogs found in school, county, and university libraries. The Web site **http://www.findarticles.com** offers quite a few links, and a selected number of them are free. Similar sites can be found at **http://www.magportal.com** and **http://www.highbeam.com/library/index.asp**.

TRACKING DOWN PRIMARY SOURCES

One of the best places to look for primary sources, both pictures and text, is the Library of Congress. Its Web site, **http://www.loc.gov**, offers a wealth of information on different historical periods and important people. The library runs the American Memory project, which is a collection of digitized documents, photographs, recorded sound, moving pictures, and text from its collection.

Here are a few other places to try while you're on the hunt for primary sources:
http://www.lib.washington.edu/subject/History/RUSA offers information on primary sources and provides links to primary source collections online.

http://www.uidaho.edu/specialcollections/Other.Repositorie s.html is a good jumping-off point for your search as it has links to collections of primary sources across the United States and around the world.

While printed material is great, make sure your resources are current. It's easy to assume that any book you use is up to date, but for some topics, even two years old is too old. Open the book and check the copyright date. On some topics, such as Greek archaeology, a book that's ten years old isn't a problem. On others, like cloning, it can be a catastrophe.

See It and Hear It for Yourself

Today you can find information in a wealth of different formats. Want to write an essay on an endangered species whose population is rebounding? You might be able to find a documentary on the animal. Check your library's video collection. Besides visiting your library, take a look at the upcoming shows on educational television channels, such as **PBS**, **National Geographic**, and **Discovery**. They may have a show coming up that suits your needs perfectly.

Don't forget books on tape and on CD. It might be more inspiring to hear FDR's speech on Pearl Harbor than to read it. This will get your brain jump-started on your persuasive essay about the causes of World War II.

TIP FILE

When using books for your research, the index in the back of the book can become your new best friend. If you are looking up a certain person, event, or place, for example, don't wade through chapters that don't contain relevant information. Go right to the index and see where your topic is discussed in the book. The table of contents in the front can be an invaluable tool too. Both of these features will save you time and effort.

Let's Go Surfing!

The perks of using the Internet to do research are pretty clear. **You can do research at any time of day.** And online data is frequently as up to date as you can get, including news stories about events that have happened in the last five minutes. You can get access to materials that might be impossible to get even through the best interlibrary loan system. By looking at one Web site, you can often find links to others that are just as helpful—or even more so.

Remember not to get lost on the net; it's easy to do. Moira Anderson Allen, a professional writer and author of **writing.com** (Watson-Guptill Publications, 2003), says, "Research online can be addictive. It can also be seductive: It feels like working, but you may find that you're spending more time looking for information than actually writing. Sometimes, knowing how to stop researching can be more important than knowing how to start."

Remember that you aren't looking for everything ever written on your topic; you want to find enough evidence to support your thesis.

Although the Internet seems perfect to use for research, it sometimes isn't. **Remember that anyone can host a site and post information to it.** That means you may be getting your information from the eight-year-old down the block who thinks she knows the best way to build a dog house or from an eighty-year-old in Wichita who posts quotes he is pretty sure President Truman once said to him over lunch.

GET CONNECTED

Check your library for its connections to online databases. Simply by entering your library card number, you can access databases that specialize in biographical information, science, and much more.

For biographies, you could look for the **Biography Resource Center**. For science, you could try the *New Book of Popular Science.*

Many libraries will even let you access their databases from home using your library card number.

"One of the most feared expressions in modern times is, 'The computer is down.'"
—Norman Augustine (1935–)

Keeping Your Facts Straight Online

Before using the facts you find online, make sure they are facts. Here are some guidelines to help you:

- Is the Web site selling anything? If so, the information may be biased to encourage your purchase.

- Does the site's URL end in .com, .org, .edu, or .gov? Some .com sites can be quite reliable while some .edu sites may not be, but as a general rule, the .org (organization), .edu (education) and .gov (government) URLs are the best ones to use.

- Does the site list sources so you know where the original information came from?

- What are the authors' or site owners' credentials?

- What does the site look like? If it is full of glitter, flash, and tinny-sounding songs, it might not be the best choice for finding facts.

- When was the site created? When was it last updated? Often this information appears at the bottom of a Web page.

For a compare and contrast essay on tornadoes and hurricanes, you could go online and find the National Oceanic and Atmospheric Administration or the Federal Emergency Management Agency and get links to other helpful resources. You might even find stories by those who witnessed these weather events firsthand.

Extraordinary Sources

Straight from the Source: The Interview

One of the best ways to do research is by actually talking to people. Books and Web sites are great sources of information, but being able to ask your questions directly to a knowledgeable person and get helpful answers in return is even better. If you find a biography of a person who works in disaster relief, you can get some great stuff. If you could personally interview that same person, you could get some incredible stuff.

Who can you interview? Here are just a few of the possible ideas:

friends   teachers

family   classmates

organization members

professionals

community leaders

While interviewing, you aren't just reading about something, you are discussing the topic with an expert. You are interacting with him or her in a way that reading just cannot provide. Before you set up an interview, review these general tips:

- **Never ask questions that can be answered with "yes" or "no."** If you do, that is the only answer you will get. How can you write something based on that? You want to avoid questions like "Do you enjoy your job?" Ask, "What is the best part of your job?" or "What are some of the challenges you face in your job?"

- **Do your homework before you interview someone**. Know the specialized vocabulary of the topic as well as possible so you don't have to keep asking for definitions while your interviewee talks. If he or she does use a term you don't know, however, ask right away for some clarification or a definition. I have interviewed dozens of physicians in my years as a writer, and I almost always have to deal with terms that are eight syllables long. Rather than interrupt and say, "What does that mean?" and, "How do you spell that?" I make sure I already have a working idea of what I might encounter while discussing a topic. I can always look up the spelling later.

- **Have your list of questions already prepared before you contact the person.** Don't make them up as you go, but also be open to asking additional questions you hadn't planned on as follow-ups to answers. If you ask a search and rescue worker what he or she dislikes the most about the job and he or she responds with, "The calls you can never be prepared for," don't stop there. Find out more about those calls!

- **Don't be afraid of the famous.** If you actually get the chance to interview someone famous, don't let his or her fame overwhelm you into not being able to speak clearly.

- **During any kind of an interview, pay attention.** If your attention drifts, you will lose important information, and the person you are talking to will notice your preoccupation.

- **As the person speaks to you, take good notes.** You can do this by either using traditional shorthand, creating your own version of shorthand, or recording the interview. Some people are uncomfortable being recorded, so always ask if this is okay first. If you have to take notes by hand, make sure to maintain eye contact throughout the interview.

- **Ask a wrap-up question.** Before you end the interview, add one last question: "Are there any other comments you would like to make that I have not covered here?" You may get a simple "no" answer, which means you did your job well. You may get a "yes" and find out some gems of info you hadn't known to ask about.

- **When you get done with the interview, go back and highlight or star the best quotes.** These are the ones that stood out as exciting or funny or just ones that will best support one of your major points.

Once your interview is complete, you will need to take your notes (or tapes) and turn them into an essay. Some writers do this with a traditional question-and-answer format. Others incorporate the responses into the text at the right spots. When it is time to write your paper, go back to those starred quotes and comments. These will be the ones you blend into your paper as you write it.

TIP FILE

For interviews, do as professional journalists do. Call to set up a time for the interview. Always ask the interview subject when would be a convenient time for him or her to talk. This shows respect and gives you time to prepare for the interview.

Three Types of Interviews

E-mail

The least personal way of conducting an interview is by
e-mail. On the other hand, since you can print a hard
copy of the e-mail, you don't have to take notes, and you
have something to refer to if you forget something.

Telephone

This is a more personal way to conduct an interview.
Over the phone, you will be able to hear tone of voice,
to get clarification on any answers given, and to follow
up instantly on any interesting statements.

In Person

Obviously, the most personal way to conduct an interview is to meet a person face to face to ask questions.
(I know you know this, but don't meet a stranger alone
anytime, anywhere. Have a parent or other adult go
with you, and meet in a public place.) While it can be a
bit intimidating, the personal interview can be the most
effective method of gathering information.

Survey Says: Take a Poll

Just as an interview can get you extraordinary quotes, creating your own survey is a great way to generate your own statistics. Develop a list of questions. Keep it short, no more than three to five questions. For a process essay on how to train a dog to load a dishwasher, you can ask people whether they have a dog, how many tricks they have taught the dog, and the like. For a persuasive essay, you can even test out your thesis with a survey. Find out what percentage of your fellow students agree with you. For example, you could ask every student in ninth grade if they think the cafeteria should offer vegetarian choices on the daily menu. Use what you learn from the survey in your paper to argue one position or the other.

As with professional surveys, **you always want to mention the number of people who participated when presenting your results.** If you only asked one person, and he or she said "Yes," you have a response of 100 percent for "Yes," but that's not a valid statistic.

Research is an important part of your essay. Whether it plays a small or large part in this assignment, make sure you do it thoroughly and well. Remember the words of Jim Bishop, author of **The Day Lincoln Was Shot.** "Assuming all authors have a flair for a well-honed phrase," he wrote, "the difference between the winners and the losers is research, the digging of facts."

BRAIN JAM:
Sharpen Your Research Skills

Prep for an interview. Imagine you've scored a 15-minute telephone interview with a famous author, scientist, military leader, or pop culture icon. (Living or dead, it doesn't matter. This is imaginary, remember?) Develop several subjects to cover in the interview (for example, professional successes and challenges, childhood, beginning of career, first successes and failures, current projects). Create five to ten questions for each subject area.

Make better notes. Paraphrasing, or putting information into your own words, is a very important skill in researching. Take a news article from today's newspaper and look for direct quotes and specific facts. Now rewrite these passages as if you were saying them aloud. Good paraphrases should sound like something you would say yourself. Ask a friend to do the same. Share your rewrites with each other and discuss any differences.

Review your research

support your th

Make a:

Forget about grammar
and spelling for the mo

Get your ideas down

ll in the details
ur outline.

FRANKLIN
CHAPTER 3
WATTS

THINK OUT OF THE BOX

Tackling the First Draft

Tackling the First Draft

When starting an essay, it's best to have a plan. Get out the box with all of your notes, tapes, magazine clippings, and other sources of inspiration and information. It's time to start building your essay.

Review all the material you gathered, and start sorting it out. Most likely, you will find that you have a lot more information than you actually need. This is good—it's much easier to cut out than stretch out! Make three stacks: information that is essential to your paper (it supports the main points); information that is good but not necessary (it gives additional information to support the details), and information that is not truly needed (it gives information that does not directly relate to any of the main points). Start with the first stack. It is what you will use for the next step.

Make Your Own Blueprint

Imagine a construction company preparing to build a skyscraper. The sketch (idea) is in hand. The tools (research) are on site. The workers need a blueprint to tell them what goes where. With your essay, you also need a blueprint. It's called an outline.

Creating an outline is not difficult. How it is organized will depend on the type of essay you are writing, but most of them follow the same basic format. Here is an example of an outline for a typical five-paragraph descriptive essay. Note that this one is written out in complete sentences. You can just use phrases if you want. I prefer this method, because when I go to write the first draft, those sentences are ready and waiting for me to cut and paste into place.

I am fortunate enough to live near one of the world's largest bookstores. If I were going to write an essay to describe it, the outline on the next page is how I would approach it.

48

ESSAY

This is the tentative title; it may change later.

A World of Books

The first line of your outline will be the essay's thesis statement (underlined). This is the main point of your essay: Everything centers on it.

INTRODUCTION:
Walking into Powell's City of Books in downtown Portland, Oregon, is like entering a world specifically designed to shelter bookworms. It has two floors, nine color-coded rooms, more than a million books, and a map to show you where you're going.

In paragraph 1, you will write about the first supporting detail of your statement.

BODY:
Paragraph 1: Taking up an entire city block, Powell's two floors cover more than 68,000 square feet, and almost every one of them is a book lover's delight.

Paragraph 2: Each room is assigned a color, from rose and gold to purple and orange.

In this paragraph, you write about the second supporting detail.

Paragraph 3: Between new and used books, more than a million books fill the maze of this reader's paradise, and everyone needs a map to find his or her way back out.

CONCLUSION:
A trip to Powell's City of Books is an overwhelming pleasure with its limitless choices. The only thing that suffers is perhaps your wallet.

SAMPLE OUTLINE

Here is the third supporting detail.

The conclusion is the place where you wrap the essay up with a summarizing statement.

49

Writing the First Draft

Using the outline created earlier, we can write the first draft:

SAMPLE FIRST DRAFT

A World of Books

Walking into Powell's City of Books in downtown Portland is like entering a world specifically designed to shelter bookworms. It has two floors, nine color-coded rooms, over a million books, and a map to show you where you're going. Although I visit it quite often, I still have to glance at the map or I wind up in the deli instead of the history room. ← **thesis statement**

Taking up an entire city block, Powell's two floors cover 68,000 square feet, and almost every one of them is a book lover's delight. Short flights of stairs connect the floors and often remind me of a maze where you are no longer sure if you are going up or coming down. To truly explore this store, most people plan to spend several hours and may even bring along a sack lunch. ← **first supporting statement**

Each one of the rooms is assigned a color, from rose and gold to purple and orange. Children of all ages head straight for the rose room, but so do automobile enthusiasts. Science-fiction fans explore the gold room, along with those who like horror and mysteries. Some rooms even include journals, art, greeting cards, calendars, and Powell's own merchandise, such as T-shirts, hats, and coffee mugs. ← **second supporting statement**

Between new and used books, more than a million books fill the maze of this reader's paradise, and everyone needs a map to find his or her way back out. A wrong turn can mean ending up at the political section, when you intended to go to look at cookbooks. Thankfully, overhead signs let you know which topics will be found in the rooms, and individual signs at each aisle break it down even further. ← **third supporting statement**

A trip to Powell's City of Books is an overwhelming pleasure with its limitless choices. For me, the biggest challenge is eliminating titles so that I can actually carry them from the store to my car. If you are like me, the only thing that suffers is perhaps your wallet. ← **conclusion**

BRAIN JAM:
First Draft

Try working in reverse. Take an essay that you like or one that you had to read for class. Identify the thesis, find the supporting details, and locate the conclusion. Now use these elements to create an outline for the essay.

Learn from the pros. Go to a bookstore or library and look for one of the titles in the Best American Essays book series. Pick a few essays to read. While you read, take notes on your reaction to the text. Were you intrigued by the opening paragraph? What is the author trying to prove or show in his or her essay? How is this point of view supported? What kinds of evidence are offered?

Watch your language. Take a look at one of your old essays and make a list of action words and descriptive words you use. Make a mark next to a word each time it is used. After you've gone through the essay, review your findings. Make a second list of words you've used four or five times and find two or three alternatives you can use next time.

good trans

a memorable clo

Your Final

a strong ope

a well-supported argum

THE SPIN ROOM

Revising Your Way to Extraordinary

Revising Your Way to Extraordinary

With draft in hand, let's look for ways to liven up that essay. There are three essential parts to an essay: the beginning (introduction), the middle (body), and the end (conclusion). There are several different ways to tackle these elements to make them extraordinary.

The Beginning . . .

It's time for that all-important first paragraph. If it does not hook the reader's attention, you can bet the rest of your essay will never get read. As you come up with that leading paragraph, think about your audience for a moment. Picture your teacher at home. It's late. Eyes are tired, and the mind is numbed by reading two hundred high-school essays. What are you going to write that will grab his or her attention? An extraordinary beginning lures the reader; it captivates and intrigues him or her.

Ernest Hemingway, when asked what was the most frightening thing he ever encountered, answered, "A blank sheet of paper."

Here are the three don'ts of writing an introductory paragraph for your essay. Do not begin with:

- **an announcement:** *I am going to write about . . .*
  or *This paper is on . . .*

- **a definition:** *According to my research . . .*
  or *The dictionary says . . .*

- **an apology or uncertainty:** *I'm not sure about this . . .*
  or *I think sometimes . . .*

Your opening has two jobs:

First, it has to let the reader know what your essay is going to be about. In other words, it's time to unveil your thesis.

Second, it has to grab the reader and reel him or her in like a fish caught on a hook after swallowing some bait.

There are several ways to do this. For example, you can start with a story. **This is called an anecdotal beginning.** Everyone loves stories. In Ellen Goodman's article, "Work Ethic Should Come with a Time Limit," she uses this method.

EXTRAORDINARY ANECDOTAL BEGINNING

There is an old story about the time Jack Kennedy was campaigning in West Virginia. One day the senator was confronted by a coal miner with a question. "Is it true," the man asked, "that you haven't done an honest day of hard labor in your life?" The would-be president abashedly admitted as much and waited for the blow. But the coal miner shook his hand and replied, "Believe me, you haven't missed a thing."

Another way to start your paper is with an unexpected statement. In Erma Bombeck's essay "Is There a Draft in Your Open Marriage," she starts this way:

EXTRAORDINARY UNEXPECTED OPENING

My son, Jaws II, had a habit that drove me crazy. He'd walk to the refrigerator-freezer and fling both doors open and stand there until the hairs in his nose iced up. After surveying two hundred dollars' worth of food in varying shapes and forms he would declare loudly "There's nothing to eat."

A third way to open your paper is with a question. A question just asks the reader to answer it, and then to continue reading. For example, look at the difference between "The mayor of the city is considering enforcing a curfew for anyone under the age of eighteen" and "Do you want to be home every night by 10 P.M.? The mayor wants to make sure you are." Or perhaps "Once again, Lance Armstrong has won the Tour de France," compared to "Can you imagine the incredible feeling of not only winning a battle with cancer, but also winning the most important bicycle race in the world for the sixth year in a row?"

The Middle: The Heart of the Essay

The purpose of the middle of your essay is simple: to support the beginning. In the opening, you made a statement. The middle is your chance to support it. You may support your thesis with stories, facts, illustrations, or other ideas. In a process essay, this is where you introduce each one of the steps. In a persuasive essay, this is where you build your argument, point by point. In a descriptive essay, this is where you provide the sensory details. In a comparison and contrast essay, this is where you discuss the similarities and/or the differences. The beginning and ending are important, but the middle is the "meat." This is where your essay will come together or fall apart.

TIP FILE

Don't let yourself fall into the trap of finding the perfect title before you begin writing. Later on, you can scan your essay to see what phrases pop out at you.

Look at these two examples of the middle of two persuasive essays. What is the difference between them?

SAMPLE PERSUASIVE ESSAY

ORDINARY MIDDLE

Movies often do not cast the right people in the roles. They frequently do not match up with what the reader imagined while reading a book. They may be too old or too tall; sometimes they just do not have the right look for that specific part.

Movies have time limits so they usually cut out a lot of the most important parts of the story. Complete scenes and conversations are cut, and this is always disappointing.

A lot of times, movies change important details about the story line. If you are a big fan of a book, this is frustrating. You do not want them to alter events.

Interesting opinions, but need facts to back them up

Here are two examples of persuasive essays on the same topic: Whenever a movie is made from a book, the book is almost always better. These examples are from the middle section, or body, of these essays. Read each example and try to find the difference between the ordinary and the extraordinary.

EXTRAORDINARY MIDDLE

Movies often do not cast the right people in the roles. They frequently do not match up with what the reader imagined while reading a book. They may be too old or too tall, sometimes they just do not have the right look for that specific part. When Tom Cruise was cast as the lead in *Interview with a Vampire*, for example, fans of Anne Rice books organized to protest because they felt he was the wrong person for the role.

strong fact

Movies have time limits so they usually cut out a lot of the most important parts of the story. Complete scenes and conversations are cut, and this is always disappointing. For example, in the recent *Harry Potter* and *Lord of the Rings* movies, parts of the story lines were chopped because they were already extremely long movies. While many people would never notice, true followers were saddened to see favorite moments eliminated.

excellent supporting detail

A lot of times, movies change important details about the story line. If you are a big fan of a book, this is frustrating. You do not want them to alter events. In the movie *Holes*, based on a book with the same title, one of the characters' lives takes a completely different direction in the film than it did in the book.

strong example

What is the main difference between these essays? If you guessed that the extraordinary one included individual examples to support the points being made, you are correct. This made each detail stronger and also made the essay much more interesting.

The Ending: Wrapping up Your Essay

Research has shown that readers remember the very last thing they read best of all. Because of this, your essay should have a killer closing that makes an impression. It should remind your reader of what the essay was about without repeating the thesis statement verbatim. You want your conclusion to build upon your original thesis.

Here are the three don'ts of writing a concluding paragraph for your essay. Do not end with:

- the introduction of any new ideas
- a repetition of the thesis statement word-for-word
- an announcement that says anything like:

  I am now writing the conclusion . . .
  or *So, in the end . . .*

BRAIN JAM:
Final Draft

Read it backward. Start at the end of your paper and read to the beginning. While it may sound odd, it's a great way to catch typos you may have missed from reading it from beginning to end so many times.

Be a word collector. Keep a small notebook with you while you read anything, from magazines to your latest history assignment, and jot down any words that stand out or look unfamiliar. Review your notebook when working on your essays and see if you can work in any of these interesting words.

Think visuals. If you've got a five-page essay due on Shakespearean sonnets, your teacher probably doesn't want you to waste a page on a portrait of William. But there are other ways to make your essay more eye-catching. Add a title page with a graphic. Make a collage to use as a cover. Make a book jacket. Add an appendix with relevant charts and graphs.

Use sensory language

create descripti

illus

Keep a folder o

use poetic tool

Structu

WRITING DESCRIPTIVE ESSAYS

And You Are There!

Writing Descriptive Essays

Many years ago, there was a radio show that would reenact famous scenes from history. The announcer would say in a dramatic voice, "And YOU . . . ARE THERE!" The whole point of the show was to make listeners feel like they were personally experiencing a historic moment. When you write a descriptive essay, you are trying to do the same thing. Instead of voices and sound effects, however, you have limitless words to paint pictures with. Are you ready to create a masterpiece?

The key to writing a descriptive essay is using sensory language. You need to use words that will engage the reader's eyes, ears, nose, tongue, and fingers. When we look at anything, from an old cactus plant to our dirty laundry, we are using all of our senses. To make your essay come alive in the mind of the reader, you must use all of those senses, too. You need to show color, invoke sounds and sensations, and provide aromas. An extraordinary descriptive essay also looks to engage the reader's emotions and feelings.

TIP FILE

There are descriptions all around you. Take out some of your favorite books and start flipping through them. Look at how these authors describe people, places, and things. Write some of these passages down on note cards and put them in your project box, or write them on a sticky note and place them near your work area.

And a left . . . and a right . . .

Keep It Moving

In Tom Kealey's essay "Bones," he writes a descriptive paragraph about a fifteen-year-old female boxer that leaves you gasping for air and sweating when you're done reading it. Here's an excerpt:

Helen, fifteen, throws a hook from her left foot, covers her midsection, ducks, takes a hit on her padded head-gear, feints with the left again, listens to her trainer's voice, mumbled by his mouthpiece, move back and back in, keep me in the center, I'll kill you near the ropes. Move with your feet, keep your waist straight. Next time you lean back, I'll knock you down; and when she does lean back, he does knock her down, with a strong hook to her forehead and a sudden shove of hips. After the fall, she stares at the tube of fluorescent lights above the gym, the glow of the street lamp through the windows, the night bugs outside. She presses her gloves against the canvas, feels the cold lick of sweat against her T-shirt.

Do you see the words that help convey the passion of this moment? Look at the verbs: "ducks," "feints," "listens," "mumbles," and "shove." You can hear the trainer's voice, feel the punches, see the street lamp.

Wake Up the Reader's Senses

Ernest Hemingway, a writer whose personal life was almost as colorful as his writing, wrote a descriptive essay called "Pamplona in July" in 1923. Note how he taps into sensory language. Do you see the colors? Feel the beat of the drum?

EXTRAORDINARY DESCRIPTION

Really beautiful girls, gorgeous, bright shawls over their shoulders, dark, dark-eyed, black-lace mantillas over their hair, walk with their escorts in the crowds that pass from morning until night along the narrow walk that runs between inner and outer belts of café tables under the shade of the arcade out of the white glare of the Plaza de la Constitución. All day and all night there is dancing in the streets. Bands of blue-shirted peasants whirl and lift and swing behind a drum, fife and reed instruments in the ancient Basque Riau-riau dances. And at night there is the throb of the big drums and the military band as the whole town dances in the great open square of the Plaza.

He uses colors ("bright shawls," "black-lace mantillas," "white glare," "blue-shirted peasants") to help guide the reader's mental picture of the scene. The use of active verbs like "whirl," "lift," "swing," and "dance" conveys a sense of movement and activity.

Remember those funny terms you learned during the poetry unit in English? It's time to freshen up your memory of them because using them is an important part of writing an effective descriptive essay.

Simile

Comparison of two unlike things using the words "like" or "as"

The sun crept over the horizon like a cat sneaking up on an unsuspecting mouse.

Metaphor

Comparison of two unlike things

The puppy was a bagful of limitless energy.

Alliteration

Repetition of the same initial consonant sounds

We loaded our sandy selves into the crowded car.

Onomatopoeia

Use of words that sound like what they mean

The thunder boomed and crashed as the cars whizzed by on the highway.

Get Ready ... Get Set ... Describe!

First, choose a topic that is worthy of being described. It should be something readers will want to know more about, and it should be connected to something you can see, smell, hear, taste, and touch. **Then, create a thesis statement that tells the reader what you are going to describe as well as your attitude toward it.** Think about how differently someone terrified of rats would describe the rodents compared with someone who keeps rats as pets and loves them. Your reader needs to know from which angle you are approaching the topic.

Three Ways to Organize

The descriptive essay has a fairly simple structure. **There are three methods of organization for this type of essay:**

1 Chronological

2 Spatial

3 Order of importance

Chronological order is in time order. If you are describing an event, this would probably be the best structure to use. Spatial order is moving from one place to another. If you are writing about your bedroom, for example, you might start on one side and move to the other in your descriptions. If you choose to write your essay in order of importance, you will most likely describe the most important detail last.

Once you have figured out the best organizational method, start compiling your details. Make a list of what you want to include and the best adjectives and adverbs to do so. Now you're ready to start writing!

Learn from EXamples

Let's pretend that you have been assigned to write a descriptive essay about someone you know well. Here is an ordinary essay next to an extraordinary one. What are the main differences between them?

ORDINARY	EXTRAORDINARY
My best friend Trish is very tall, with long legs and soft, short hair. She likes to tell jokes and has a great laugh. Trish likes to eat peppermint candies, and I can smell them when I pass her in the hallway between classes. Although I have only known Trish for a year, I think we will be best friends for the rest of our lives.	My best friend Trish is quite tall, with legs as long as her hair is short. She often refers to herself as a giraffe with a buzz cut. She likes to tell jokes and has a great laugh that seems to start way down in her toes and work itself up. By the time it reaches her mouth, it explodes with a snort and a gasp that makes me laugh, too. Trish is always munching on red and white peppermint candies that crinkle when she unwraps them. She smells like my favorite toothpaste when I pass her in the hallway between classes. Although I have only known Trish for a year, I think we will be best friends for the rest of our lives.

Uses strong visual images

Now you can hear the laugh

Evokes the sense of smell

Let's imagine you have to describe a place. If you live in the Pacific Northwest, like I do, one of the first places that might come to mind is Mt. Hood. Here is an example of an ordinary and extraordinary description of that mountain. Again, what are the main differences between the two?

ORDINARY	EXTRAORDINARY
Mt. Hood is very large. You can see it from virtually every place in Portland, although it is often covered by clouds. There is snow on the top almost all year round. From my home, it looks like I should be able to climb to the top in a matter of minutes. I would stand on the summit and smell the clean snow and feel the cold wind blow against me.	Although Mt. Hood is a huge mountain, I had lived in Oregon for more than a month before I first spotted it. I arrived in the autumn, and each day was heavy with gray clouds that blanketed the mountain, and so I never suspected it was there. One bright morning, I looked up and gasped. Gleaming like a golden, snow-covered dome in the warm morning sunlight was this monolith. Closing my eyes, I could just imagine standing at the top, feeling the pine-scented wind blowing against me. I opened my eyes and welcomed my new friend.

the visual imagery creates strong impression

uses "pine-scented" to add smell

a vivid dream	circus animals
a thunderstorm	the way you spend your favorite holiday
your house's basement or attic	
	a music concert
your favorite piece of art	having the hiccups
a person who loves nature	a famous moment in history

Think of something you would like to write a descriptive essay about. Let's imagine you want to write about the ocean. You could start with this:

*The waves rush in toward the sandy shore.
Each one is topped by white foam like too many
soap suds in the shower.*

Next, you could bring in the sounds of the waves, the smell of the coastal air, and even the taste of salt on your lips. To make it extraordinary, however, why not try describing the ocean from the viewpoint of a seagull? A surfer? A child? What if it was an ocean on another planet? What if the time was one thousand years ago or one thousand years in the future?

Pick another topic. How about if you want to describe a rock concert that you attended? How would you start if you were describing it chronologically? Perhaps you would start with your arrival at the venue or the notes of the first song. Why not try starting at the end of the concert and working backwards? If you were describing it spatially, you could describe the audience, then the stage, and finally the band. If you chose to describe it by order of importance, you could start with the clothes people were wearing and move onto the band and finally onto the rock star you came to see in the first place.

Remember, the key to writing a good descriptive essay is making your readers feel like they are experiencing something right along with you. What amazing things have you felt, seen, heard, or tasted in your life? What was the best day of your life? The worst? Any of these could make a terrific essay. Just imagine that announcer in your mind saying, "And YOU . . . ARE THERE!"

PROJECT JUMP START

★ **Pick an object and write about it in descriptive terms.** Do not name what the object is anywhere in the essay. Compare or contrast it to things using similes and metaphors. Talk about its taste, smell, sound, or shape, but never name it. Have several other people read the essay and see what they guess the object is. How close did they come to guessing it correctly?

★ **Pick a common event**—a rainstorm, someone cooking in the kitchen, a phone conversation—and write about it only from the auditory sense. In other words, describe it all in terms of the sounds it makes. What details can you come up with that you might not have thought of before?

BRAIN JAM:
Get Descriptive!

Take an alien point of view. Imagine that you're an alien that just landed on this planet and write a scene where you witness an everyday event, such as students entering their school or people stuck in a traffic jam.

Pick a sense. Try writing a paragraph about a person, place, or thing using only one of your five senses. For example, how would you describe your desk using only the sense of touch? How would you describe a park using only your sense of smell?

Read all about it. Grab the latest issue of your favorite magazine and find an interview. How does the article give you a sense of who the subject is? Make a list of all the words and phrases used to describe the person featured.

Pick a topic you a

First things first
start with the first step
finish with the final step

Make a list of steps a

transition

Have someone read your paper
see if anything needs further

WRITING PROCESS
ESSAYS

Been There,
Done That

Writing Process Essays

If you have ever had to put an item together and struggled to make heads or tails of the directions (Part B goes into what slot?), you know what it is like when a process essay goes wrong. **A process essay is a how-to paper; it is a chance to explain how something is done.** It is an essay that tells you to throw away your fancy adverbs and adjectives and concentrate on those cold, hard facts. Readers don't want to know if the screwdriver they should use has a glittering blue handle. They need to know if they need a flat-head or a Phillips-head screwdriver.

Some process essays consist of step-by-step directions. They are designed to instruct or inform the reader. They show that you know how to break things down into a logical process. Process essays can also include the why and the how behind a process. They can address an issue as simple as playing catch or as complicated as dealing with global warming. They can discuss how your neighborhood began a recycling program or how your uncle Fred started his own llama ranch or how to do tricks on your skateboard.

The key to writing good process essays is making them exceptionally clear and well thought out. In order to do that, you have to be familiar and comfortable with the topic, either because you are an expert on it or because you have done some careful research.

When you are writing a process essay, it is important to use the right transition words to move the steps along and keep them all connected. Try these:

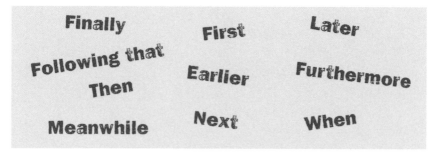

Finally   First   Later

Following that   Earlier   Furthermore

Then

Meanwhile   Next   When

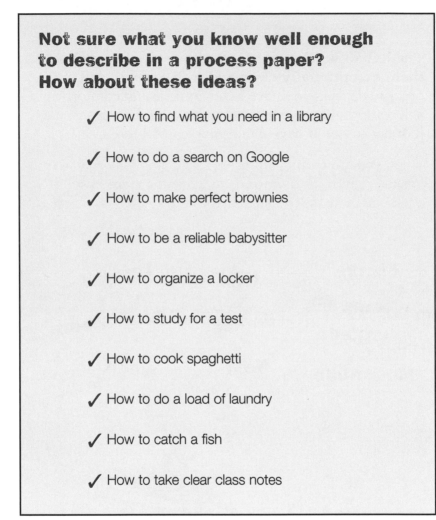

Not sure what you know well enough to describe in a process paper? How about these ideas?

✓ How to find what you need in a library

✓ How to do a search on Google

✓ How to make perfect brownies

✓ How to be a reliable babysitter

✓ How to organize a locker

✓ How to study for a test

✓ How to cook spaghetti

✓ How to do a load of laundry

✓ How to catch a fish

✓ How to take clear class notes

When you are choosing your topics, ask yourself whether it is a process that is better described with visuals rather than with words. For example, instructions for building a model require visuals. Reading about it just will not suffice. Also check to see if this topic is something that would take a whole manual to explain. If so, it's too complicated a topic for an essay. Once you have your topic, make sure it is focused by writing it into a thesis statement: "In this paper, I will explain how to _____."

Next, make a list of the steps involved. At first, you can just jot them down as they occur to you. When you can't think of any more, start putting them in sequential order. Before long, you will find some that you overlooked. **All process essays are put in chronological order,** so make sure your steps are in the correct sequence (first step to last step).

Last, make a list of specialized terms you might use in your process paper. Make sure you clearly define each one within the text. It's easy to use technical words without thinking about it because to us, they are familiar. Have someone who does not know anything about your topic read your paper. Does he or she get stuck on a word or get lost between one step and another? These are clues that you need to go back and rewrite.

Ready to show your readers how to do something? When you start your essay, it is vital that you find a way to show your readers why this process could be important to them. For example, let's say you are going to write about the procedure for washing a dog. Your essay begins as follows:

ORDINARY	EXTRAORDINARY
Giving a dog a bath can be challenging. There are only five basic steps involved, however, and then the job is done.	One of the best summer jobs for teenagers is walking and taking care of dogs. This often includes giving the dogs a bath. Although that is not always easy, it can be done in five basic steps.

Now a great many readers will have a reason for wanting to find out how to wash a dog.

Beyond Step by Step

Sometimes a process essay takes the reader behind the scenes to show why and how something works. For your biology class, you may need to write a paper on photosynthesis in plants. For a history class, your process essay should more than just list the steps used in mummification; you're going to want to explain how the process works.

ORDINARY

In ancient Egypt, people sometimes were made into mummies as part of a burial ritual. First, the internal organs of the dead person were removed. Then the body and the organs were treated with natron. Then the body was left to dry for thirty-five to forty days. After drying, the body cavities were filled with spices and herbs and oils and gums were rubbed on the skin. Then the body was wrapped in linen, decorated with jewelry, and covered in resin.

EXTRAORDINARY

At first, ancient Egyptians buried their dead in the sand. The hot, dry climate of their lands caused the bodies to naturally dry up, or become mummified. Later, the Egyptians developed their own method for preserving a body, a process now known as mummification. The Egyptians believed mummification would protect the body for eternity.

How a dead person was mummified would vary based on his or her position in society. A ruler would receive the most elaborate treatment. First the organs would be removed from the deceased's body. The body cavity and the organs were treated with natron, a type of salt to help dry them out. It usually took about thirty-five to forty days for the body to dry out. It was important to dry the body out to prevent it from rotting.

The ordinary example is an okay description, but it doesn't really explain how mummification works or why the ancient Egyptians did it.

In the extraordinary version, the reader has a more complete understanding of the process of mummification. He or she gains some insight into ancient Egyptian culture and science while learning the process.

Process essays are hard to keep simple. Remember to give your readers a reason to follow the process, and then logically move from one step to the next. Assume your readers don't have a clue about your topic, and include each step, define each word, and point out each tool. You're the expert.

PROJECT JUMP START

Pick something you do every day (brushing your teeth, riding your bike, reading a book, etc.). Write out the steps involved from beginning to end. Make sure you include every single detail. Go over it and see if you missed any steps. If so, go back and add them, and then write them out as an essay.

Ask someone to explain to you how to do something you do not currently know how to do (within reason). As they tell you, write down the steps. Would you be able to do the activity after reading the steps? Did your instructor forget a step or four? Did he or she use terms that were unfamiliar to you? Use this experience to help you write a better process essay.

Look behind the scenes of a natural phenomenon and write a process essay on how and why it happens. How does lightning happen? Why does the earth sometimes quake?

BRAIN JAM:
Getting a Handle on Processes

Take some expert advice. Watch an instruction-al program on TV and take notes on how the instructions are conveyed. How are the instruc-tions presented visually? What is the relationship between the spoken words and the images?

Read the instructions. There are instructions all around you—instructions for your television, your video games, your cell phone, and even your toaster oven. Take a look at an instruction booklet for any gadget or gizmo found in your house. What types of transitional words are used? Does the order of the steps make sense? Did you find it easy to read? If not, what would you do to make the booklet simpler?

similarities

Be sure to choose t
method for illustra
points.

ave strong suppor

onclusion.

Make sure you
cient points

WRITING COMPARE AND CONTRAST ESSAYS

Making a Comparison

Hmm . . . Chimps have fur
. . . Apples have skin . . .

Writing Compare and Contrast Essays

Have you ever stood in a store and compared two video games? You might have compared their stories, characters, special features, and prices before making a decision to purchase one. You might be standing in the kitchen one morning, noticing how many similarities there are between your father and the oak tree in the front yard. You compare and contrast things every day. You look to see what they have in common and how they are different. The same thing can be done in an essay.

The compare and contrast essay does one of two things:

It can show the similarities between two unlike things, such as chimps and apples.

It can show the differences between two similar things, such as typewriters and computer keyboards.

So what's the point of this type of essay? Simple. It's intended to help you develop your critical and analytical thinking skills as well as your essay-writing skills. In your English class, your teacher might want you to look at two poems by the same author or two stories written during the same historic period, such as the Harlem Renaissance. In physics, you might need to compare two conflicting theories about black holes.

Building a Framework

There are three ways to organize the compare and contrast essay. Let's look at an example. Let's say you were assigned to write a compare and contrast essay on being in the church choir or playing in the school band.

First, you can discuss one object in full and then discuss the other.

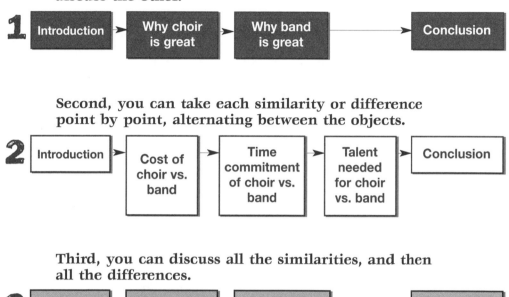

1 Introduction → Why choir is great → Why band is great → Conclusion

Second, you can take each similarity or difference point by point, alternating between the objects.

2 Introduction → Cost of choir vs. band → Time commitment of choir vs. band → Talent needed for choir vs. band → Conclusion

Third, you can discuss all the similarities, and then all the differences.

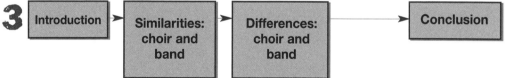

3 Introduction → Similarities: choir and band → Differences: choir and band → Conclusion

What two elements should you compare? Most likely, your teacher will let you know what he or she wants you to compare or contrast. By doing so, you will demonstrate that you have a strong knowledge of both topics. You cannot compare the causes of World War I and World War II effectively without understanding them. You cannot contrast how some plants grow from spores instead of seeds without knowing the basics of both types of plant reproduction.

When you choose a topic for this type of essay, you have to make sure you have relevant points to cover. For example, if you are going to show the similarities between two things, they should not be so dissimilar that you can't find any points of commonality. An essay about how a porcupine is similar to a bowl of tapioca pudding would be pretty hard to support. To make sure you have enough valid points, jot them down on a piece of paper first. Try to have at least three or four solid points of comparison.

Imagine that you were asked to write an essay that compares the characters of Tom Sawyer and Huckleberry Finn. What could you come up with for your list? You could divide it into looks, attitudes, and personalities. (Haven't read the book? Replace the characters with anything you want: two friends, two recipes, two favorite snacks, etc.)

You could organize the essay one of three ways: Discuss everything about Tom and then everything about Huck and then write a conclusion ("I think Tom was the more responsible of the two characters"), or talk about Tom's looks and then Huck's looks, then Tom's attitudes and Huck's attitudes, and finally Tom's personality and then Huck's personality. Then, you could write a conclusion. ("It is obvious why Huck gets into more trouble than does Tom.") Last, you could write about Tom's looks, attitudes, and personality and then Huck's looks, attitudes, and personality, and then write the conclusion. ("In the end, I think Huck would be more fun to spend time with over the summer.")

Here's an example of an essay that compares reading books to watching television.

ORDINARY	EXTRAORDINARY
I know that I am supposed to read, but I think a person learns more from watching television.	I know that some people think it is better to read, but I think some people learn more from watching television. Watching television appears to work best for me. Here's why.
Books are really long. They have a lot of words in them I don't know. It takes hours to finish reading them.	Books are often hundreds of pages long. It takes me many hours to read that much. Sometimes, I am confused by the vocabulary an author uses. I do a great deal of reading for several classes at school, and I find that my eyes get tired and my attention wanders if I read too long.
Television is easier to understand. I can watch a show about something educational, and in an hour, I have learned all I need to know.	Television entertains me and seems to be easier for me to understand. I have often watched educational television shows and have learned a lot from them. Several have helped me to better comprehend the different topics we study in school. For example, I watched a National Geographic special about astronomy, and afterwards, I did better on my science test. Television often condenses information into an hour, which is an amount of time I can usually fit into my schedule. Overall, I believe that television is the best way for me to learn new information.

interesting thesis, but not enough support

sounds like a complaint

good supporting info

PROJECT JUMP START

Imagine yourself in someone else's shoes. Compare and/or contrast a day in your life as a public-school or private-school student to what you think a day in the life of a homeschooled student is like. What are the differences? What are the similarities? Where would you go to research this topic?

Tackle characters. Compare and/or contrast a fictional character who is "street smart" with one who is "book smart." How are they different and the same? Think in terms of how each one acts and speaks, the differences in personality and background, and so on.

Look at today versus long ago. Compare and/or contrast the issues that concerned high-school students when your parents were in high school (probably the mid- to late-1970s) and the ones that concern your generation.

Think upside down. Select an idea for a compare and contrast essay, and then see what you can do to turn the idea upside down. Compare two things and take the unexpected position ("Movies are better than the books on which they are based"). Compare the best- and worst-reviewed movies of the year, and show why the worst one was better. No matter how you find a way to think outside the box, remember the foundation of your extraordinary compare and contrast essays needs to be made of facts.

BRAIN JAM:
Compare and Contrast Possibilities

Practice, practice, practice. That's one of the best ways to get better at comparing and contrasting. Pick three topics from the list of different possibilities below and create an outline for one, craft a thesis for another, and write a body paragraph for the third.

- o Artemis Fowl vs. Harry Potter
- o paper bags vs. plastic bags
- o country music vs. blues
- o tea vs. coffee
- o university vs. community college
- o scooters vs. motorcycles
- o black-and-white film vs. color film
- o standard cameras vs. digital cameras
- o public school vs. homeschool
- o modern medicine vs. alternative medicine

personal nar...
slice of your

Brainstorm and see whe

Include a lot of

Ask yourself questi

WRITING BOLD BOOK
REPORTS AND PERSONAL
NARRATIVES

EXcel at Common English Assignments

EXcel at Common English Assignments

Book reports will be required of you throughout your education. Contrary to what you may think, they aren't just assigned to make sure you actually read the book. They are assigned so that you will take what you read and connect it to the English standards you have been taught as well as to demonstrate how you took the information from the book and applied it to your life and education.

After you've done a couple of the traditional book reviews and reports, **try something that will get your teacher as excited about the book as you are.** If you have the chance to be adventurous with your book report, why not try writing the report in an entirely different way? You can design it to be like a magazine's book review, a movie review, a newspaper story, or a television commercial. Create a catchy jingle or a motto for it. Write a headline or photo captions.

The key to writing an extraordinary book report is ignoring the ordinary. Don't just list the typical information; go beyond that. **Show why the book was wonderful, terrible, inspiring, or mind-numbing.** Use some of the techniques you have learned from writing other kinds of papers. Use what you learned about writing a descriptive essay to help you describe a character. If you read a nonfiction book that taught you to do something, utilize the process essay in your book report. Utilize the research tips no matter what kind of book report you write.

Heads Up!

Jazz It Up!

Here are a few ways to spice up that book report:

- **Research the life of the author to show how his or her experiences affected the book.** It can change how you feel about a book if you know what the author's life was like. It's amazing to read *Gone with the Wind* or *To Kill a Mockingbird*, for example, and then realize that those authors never published another word! They were truly one-hit wonders.

- **Contact the author to get his or her comments and thoughts.** Many authors have their own Web sites where you can learn about them and even e-mail them questions. If fate is being extraordinarily kind, perhaps you can even conduct some kind of interview.

- **Imagine that the story has been turned into a movie.** Who would you cast in each role? What parts of the story would you include, and what parts would you leave out? Why?

- **Create a poster, flow chart, diorama, sculpture,** or other art project about some event or character in the story, and share it with the class.

- **Select your favorite passages from the story** and write them into your report. Explain why you liked them so much. What made them stand out to you? Were they the most descriptive? Shocking?

- **Imagine that you are writing a sequel to the book,** and explain what you would include in it and what would happen to the characters.

Getting Personal

Personal narratives, on the other hand, are simply stories about something that has happened in your life. It can be a defining moment, and not necessarily an autobiography that details your life from birth to present. It can be about an event, a person, or a trip. It can be about major events such as moving, the loss of a friend, receiving awards, or experiencing traumas. It can be about trivial things, such as going to a friend's house, getting a letter, going to the mall, or solving a mystery. Again, the key here is not to state dull facts ("I was born in Indiana in 1990 to Ellen and Roger Smith"), but to show who you are. You will need to include a lot of details. While the story may be old and familiar to you, it is all new to the reader.

For example, think of something that happened to you that changed you. It doesn't need to be profound. It could be discovering that you like artichokes or finding out that your great-great-great-great aunt Martha once worked on the Underground Railroad. Now set the stage. Write down everything you can remember about the event.

An ordinary essay will simply relate the story. An extraordinary essay will go far beyond that. It will provide information about the place, the time, who was there, what was happening, and why it was happening. It will include any dialogue you can remember, what music was playing, or what the weather was like. It should reflect on how the moment changed your life, your thinking, your appearance—whatever. To make the essay even richer in detail, take the time to talk to your family members or friends who were present for the event. What details do they remember?

This personal narrative is the type of essay you will eventually need to write for college, scholarship, and job applications. It is your chance to stand out, to get attention, to say, "Hey! I am a fascinating person, so take a second look."

"A narrative is like a room on whose walls a number of false doors have been painted; while within the narrative, we have many apparent choices of exit, but when the author leads us to one particular door, we know it is the right one because it opens."
—John Updike (1932–)

PROJECT JUMP START

 Write your book report in the form of a newspaper article. It should have an attention-getting headline and the most important facts at the beginning, and it should read like a news story that actually happened (regardless of whether your book was fiction or nonfiction).

 Write a diary or journal entry from the point of view of one of the characters in the book you read. Include details from the story that explain what the book is about.

 Represent what you read in some form of art. Sculpt a character, draw a sketch of a scene, paint a portrait, build a diorama, create clay models—whatever art form you like best.

Think of a moment when you surprised yourself. Perhaps you did or said something unexpected, you did better or worse than you had thought you would, or you discovered something about yourself that you did not realize before. Write out the story, including as many details as you can, like setting, dialogue, and what lesson you learned from it.

BRAIN JAM:
Revisit Your Favorites

Cruise your bookshelves and pull out a few of your all-time favorite books. For each book, ask yourself the following questions:

What is the plot?

What is the theme(s) of the book?

Who are the major characters?

Why is this book one of your favorites?

Sharing your opinion.

State your rea:

Support your opinio

Use logic and r

ose a topic or find an a

Research! Gather statisti
trations, etc. to support

Try and anticipate your re

WRITING PERSUASIVE ESSAYS

You Know I'm Right!

Writing Persuasive Essays

Everybody has opinions, and most likely you do too. The persuasive essay gives you the chance not only to share that opinion, but also to list all of your supporting reasons for having that opinion. Although this type of paper is sometimes called an argumentative paper, it's not about fighting. Instead, it's about persuading: presenting your position in such a way that your readers will naturally want to agree with you. You want them to agree with your position, accept your belief, and follow your recommended plan of action.

The persuasive paper is to the writer as the debate is to the speaker. You choose a side and then concentrate on giving evidence or reasons why you chose as you did. It requires a good amount of logic and reasoning, of course, but at the same time, it demands equal amounts of emotion and passion. You are not writing to explain something; you are writing to win people to your side of the argument.

From Topic to Thesis

For this type of essay, you may have to choose a topic from a list, find one of your own, or deal with the one assigned to you. Whatever the case may be, you want to check in with yourself about how you feel about the issue. For example, stem cell research—is it the key to medical breakthroughs or a morally flawed practice? Jot down your reasons for your opinion on a piece of paper. You want to make sure you have enough reasons and that they are solid, or backed up with facts. Don't base them on whims or something you have a hunch about but no way to prove. Chances are that if you can't think of a handful of reasons to support your position, you don't have the right topic to write about.

Once you have your list of reasons, **it's time to craft a thesis**. It should be a clear statement of your opinion. In the first draft, don't worry too much about the language of the thesis; you can refine it in your next draft. You want to have a distinct, supportable position. For example, "Student performance can be improved by starting school an hour later." There are studies that show that many teens aren't getting enough sleep and that there are physical and mental problems that can arise from a lack of sleep.

Where you put your thesis in the essay depends on your audience and your purpose. For example, if you just want them to do something simple like write a letter to the editor of a newspaper, you can lead with your opinion because there most likely will not be much disagreement. If you want your readers to accept a much more difficult idea, such as banning television, then you might want to put your statement at the end of the essay.

TIP FILE

One way to get your point across while taking your work to the next level is to go visual. Include graphs and charts with your report. Use a slide show or video to emphasize your points if you present your essay orally. These will give you credibility.

Transitional words in a persuasive essay often include:

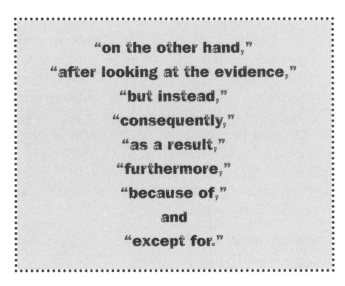

"on the other hand,"

"after looking at the evidence,"

"but instead,"

"consequently,"

"as a result,"

"furthermore,"

"because of,"

and

"except for."

The Power of Persuasion

How exactly do you win someone over to your side? This will not be as challenging as you think. In many ways, you already know how to win an argument. Have you ever tried to convince your parents of something, from letting you stay up later to getting a dog? If so, you know that **one of the best places to begin is on common ground**.

For example, if you want to go to camp during the summer, you can start with, "You know how we both agreed I needed to spend more time outside?" Move on to how those needs or wants can be met: "If I go to Camp Party-a-lot, I will be outside all day for a week."

Anticipate objections and counteract them. "I know it's expensive, but I have that $50 Aunt Gretel sent me and I can earn a little more when I babysit for the Andersons. I know it's a long way away, but I can get a ride to camp with Sally, that girl down the block who you like so much." Finally, bring it all home. "So, as you can see, camp won't be a problem at all, so let's fill out that application now."

As you prepare to write this type of essay, **take the time to think about what your readers' opinions might be**. Anticipate what they will object to, and be ready to respond to their objections with support. For example, if you are writing a paper stating that school should start one hour later in the morning, think about why some people might disagree with you. Perhaps they are worried that they will, in turn, get out of school an hour later, which might interfere with a part-time job or other regular activity. Perhaps some people might object because they like getting up early. You need to have a response built into your essay for any possible objection. Address the concern about getting out an hour later or not getting up as early as someone would like. **If you ignore objections, your position will be weakened,** and you will not have the credibility you need to persuade your readers.

If you are feeling completely without an opinion at the moment, here are some topics to argue for or against:

- uniforms in school
- increased speed limits on highways
- the death penalty
- year-round school
- who should own outer space
- infomercials
- health food
- vegetarianism
- prayer in school
- going to college

Taking Your Essay to the Next Level

Let's look at an example of the first paragraph of a persuasive essay.

ORDINARY	EXTRAORDINARY
Everybody wants children to be safe in their own homes. When families put pools in their backyards, however, it is just too big a risk. Lots of children drown each year in pools. These deaths can be prevented if only people would pay more attention. I believe that pools should be illegal for anyone who has children.	Everybody wants children to be safe in their own homes. When families put pools in their backyards, however, it can be a big risk. More than four thousand children under the age of five drown in pools each year. Amazingly, 80 percent of them are within eyesight of a parent or other caretaker at the time. Drowning can be prevented if parents install fences and have their kids wear special alarms. That would certainly be better than making pools illegal for people who have children!

The ordinary writer started off well by stating a common concern of many people. From there, things went downhill. Although she has a strong opinion and gives reasons to support it, it is not backed up with enough support.

The extraordinary opinion is the same, but the facts and examples make it clear that the opinion has merit.

Here is another example of an introductory paragraph:

ORDINARY	EXTRAORDINARY
Every year there are hundreds of car accidents involving teenagers. The age group most often involved in serious car collisions is that of teenagers. Because of this, I believe the legal driving age in this country should be raised.	In the last two years, I have had three good friends injured in car accidents. One of them will never walk again. Statistics show that more than 60 percent of the drivers involved in serious car collisions are teenagers. Because of this, I believe the legal driving age in this country should be raised from sixteen to eighteen years old.

Did you notice how in the ordinary example, the idea and stance were clear, but there was no passion? How did the writer change that in the extraordinary example? How did adding a couple of numbers also change the essay?

As you write your persuasive essay, remember to choose a position you are enthusiastic about and to support it with a combination of passion and proof. Sincerity is important, but facts will win out over it almost every time.

PROJECT JUMP START

★ **Have an opinion.** Think of a controversial issue that you have a strong opinion about. Write a persuasive essay from the opposite point of view. Argue for the side you actually disagree with. What did you learn about the topic in the process? How did it affect your opinion? What kind of research did you have to do?

★ **Think locally.** Imagine that you are writing an essay persuading students to sell candy to raise money for the school's sports teams. What points would you use to persuade them to do a good job? Write them down. Now, imagine that you are writing to an audience of neighbors that you will be asking to buy the candy. What reasons would you use to convince them to buy it? Write them down. How do the lists differ when you change audiences?

HELP WITH PERSUASION

Whether you call it an argumentive or persuasive essay, there are a number of places to turn for help online. The writing center of Texas A&M University offers some tips at its Web site.
http://uwc.tamu.edu/handouts/plan/argument.html

The AOL@School site provides a summary the persuasive essay as well as other writing resources.
http://aolatschool.factmonster.com/homework/writingskills7.html

BRAIN JAM:
Understanding Persuasion

See it from the other side. Think of an issue that you have strong feelings on. If you are definitely pro on the issue, try to put yourself in the opposing side's shoes. Write down three pieces of evidence that would support their case.

Get media savvy. Flip through a pile of magazines with a notebook and pen handy. Look at ads and make notes about the different tactics being used to persuade you to buy. Peer pressure? Big promises of fabulous results? Used by your favorite celebrities? Try to identify what types of incentives companies are employing to get you to be one of their customers.

Take a page from the politicians. For some politicians, every speech is a persuasive essay spoken aloud. Listen to a political speech twice. The first time just note what the overall point of view is and your initial emotional responses to the words. The second time through work on taking apart the argument by listing the reasons mentioned that were intended to sway you to the politician's view and the ways he or she tried to refute any opposing viewpoints.

Keep track of ti

Vivid vocabu

Legible handwriting

avoid cliche

Close attention to grammar, spelling and

Fill up the pages

A clearly designed int

Have a cle

Use strong supporti

vide transitio

WRITING ESSAYS FOR THE SATs

There's Nothing Average About That Test!

Writing Essays for the SATs

One of the times you most want to make sure you are writing a great essay is when you are taking the SATs. **Unlike most writing assignments, this one is performed under a strict time limit (25 minutes).** That means you have to know what you are doing before you get started if you want to put that pencil down before the bell rings.

Responding Promptly

The format of the SAT essay is a simple one. It begins with some kind of statement, often referred to as a prompt. It may be a well-known phrase or thought; it may be a quote or even some kind of statistic. Your job will be to respond to it appropriately. Your actual opinion does not matter; your ability to respond correctly is what is being graded.

Here are some of the types of prompts you may be asked to write to:

- Henry David Thoreau once said that it is not necessary to travel in order to learn.
- The Internet is bringing the people of the world closer together.
- To remake the world, a person must start with him/herself.
- Time is your best ally.
- The joy is in the journey.
- Reading is to the mind what exercise is to the body.

Follow the Directions

The directions for responding to the essay question are usually the same. If you read and understand them now, you can save precious time when you get to the actual test. Here is the gist of what they tell you:

- You have 25 minutes to plan and write this essay. The topic is assigned below.

- You need to focus on developing a point of view, presenting logical ideas, and using language precisely.

- Write your essay on the lines provided on the answer sheet. There is no extra paper allowed.

- Make sure your handwriting is clear and legible. (Points will be taken off if it isn't!)

- DO NOT WRITE ON ANY OTHER TOPIC than the one provided for you. (An off-topic essay gets zero, nada, nothing, zip!)

The first thing you will do after skimming those directions is to look carefully at the statement you have been assigned. Read the statement. Note what your initial response to it is. Do you agree? Disagree? Does a story or event or fact spring to mind? These are important to note because you will use them in your outline as your supporting evidence.

Get Ready!

Your essay will be graded in part on your ability to make your case. **One of the ways to an extraordinary essay on test day is to prepare examples ahead of time.** Take a sheet of paper and write "history" across the top of it. Now write the numbers 1 through 3, leaving lots of space between the numbers. By number 1, write a historic event, such as the attack on Pearl Harbor or the Lewis and Clark expedition. Then write on separate lines the answers to the following questions: when, where, what, and who. Repeat this for the next two items using a different event each time.

You will also want to prepare examples for literature, coming with examples of works, such as poems and novels, and identifying major characters, plot points, and themes. Create examples of contemporary events, too.

And don't forget your own life. **You're going to want at least three personal examples of an event, person, or book that has influenced your life in some way.** In this case, you want to generate a description, note a few key details, and describe what you learned.

TIP FILE

One thing that reviewers may consider when looking at your essay is how you write your sentences. Make sure to use a variety of sentence lengths and styles.

Remember that when it comes to this kind of essay, you are not being graded on your opinion. You are being graded on how well you write an essay supporting that opinion. Those supporting concepts can come from a number of places, including what you have learned about in one of your classes, recent news stories, literature, history, or even your own personal experience. It is essential that those examples be logical and directly related to the question you are being asked. If you get off topic, you will lose focus—and points.

As you put together your outline, keep in mind those lessons you learned earlier in the book. You must have an **introduction** (I got the point, here is my position, and now segue into the body); a **body** (2–4 paragraphs of those solid supporting details mentioned above); and a **conclusion** (tie it together, no repetition or new ideas). If you don't have all three, can you guess what happens? Right—you lose points.

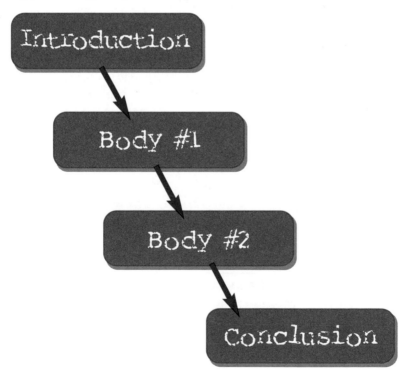

Begin Sharp, Close Strong

Since you're working with a tight time constraint, keep your introduction fairly simple and to the point. You want to acknowledge that you understand the assignment, convey your position on the assignment, and proceed with your examples.

Conclusions can also be brief, as short as two sentences. Make sure to have one; having no conclusion will lose you points. Remember that the conclusion echoes the introduction without using the same words. One way to handle this is to use your examples as your transition. For example, "These examples clearly illustrate . . ."

Taking It to the Next Level

A solid essay that sticks to the topic and has an introduction, body, and conclusion and logical supporting evidence will most likely get you four points—out of six. How do you get those extra two? As usual, by going that extra mile. In this case, that means paying attention to a few extra aspects:

- **Use lively, vivid, exciting vocabulary.** Make sure you're using and spelling the word right, though. Don't just throw in a couple of big words to look smarter. If you use them wrong, you achieve the opposite.

- **Make sure your grammar and spelling are strong.** Are your pronouns correct? Are you keeping to one point of view? Watch your verb tense— don't switch from past to present to future and back again.

- **Avoid clichés** and trite expressions that everyone uses. Be unique.

- **Include transitions** between the parts of your essay. "Meanwhile," "furthermore," "on the other hand," "next," etc. help guide the reader smoothly through your writing.

- **Fill up the pages.** Don't write huge to do so, and don't get to the bottom and scrunch to make it. Pace yourself; there is no extra paper if you go over, and a half-filled essay page does not look good.

- **Be neat.** Essays with handwriting too hard to read are given to a special department to read (now there's a fun job!). Do you want people with that job grading your essay? Think about it.

HIT THE BOOKS

Looking for more advice and some writing prompts to use for practice? Check out these books:

Mastering The New SAT Essay: Seven Simple Steps by Elizabeth Drumwright

Increase Your Score in 3 Minutes a Day: SAT Essay by Randall McCutcheon and James Schaffer

The New SAT Writing Workbook by Kaplan

Beat the Clock: A Minute-by-Minute Breakdown

Here is how the experts recommend that you spend those precious 25 minutes in order to get the essay done:

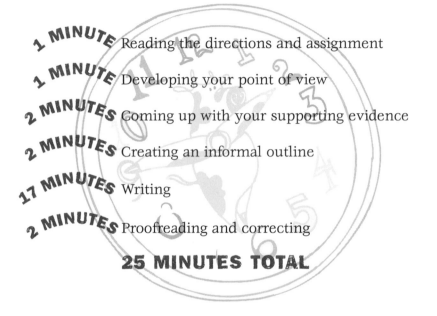

1 MINUTE Reading the directions and assignment

1 MINUTE Developing your point of view

2 MINUTES Coming up with your supporting evidence

2 MINUTES Creating an informal outline

17 MINUTES Writing

2 MINUTES Proofreading and correcting

25 MINUTES TOTAL

Here Come the Scores!

Your essay will be read by two different people, and each person will give it a score of up to 6 points (for a possible score of 12). While you may think that they are going over it with a proverbial fine-toothed comb, the truth is that they might spend three minutes (or less) reading it. You have to make a solid impression QUICK-LY. Be clear, be solid, and be strong. They can see that in mere seconds!

SAT Essay Scorecard

Once your essay has been reviewed, your work will receive a score from 6 (the best) to 0 (don't worry, the only way to get a zero is to write an essay on a completely different topic or not write an essay at all). According to the College Board, the organization that creates and administers the SATs, here's what it takes to get the top three scores:

6 equals an outstanding essay.
Essays that receive this score:
- Have a well-developed, insightful point of view.
- Show remarkable critical thinking skills.
- Provide strong supporting evidence.
- Demonstrate exceptional writing skills, such as varied sentence structure and vocabulary.

5 is for an effective essay.
Essays that receive this score:
- Have a well-developed point of view.
- Show strong critical thinking skills.
- Provide good supporting evidence.
- Exhibit strong writing skills, such as variety in sentence structure and vocabulary.

4 means a satisfactory essay.
Essays that receive this score:
- Develop a point of view.
- Show some critical thinking skills.
- Exhibit fair but somewhat inconsistent writing skills, such as varied sentence structure and appropriate vocabulary.

PROJECT JUMP START

★ **The only way to get better at the essay part of the test is to practice, practice, practice.** Write two essays using two of the following prompts:

- Does music have the ability to affect human behavior, either positively or negatively?

- Where does innovation come from? Does it come from people with brand-new ideas or from people who develop ideas that are derived from current methods of accomplishing tasks?

- Is the right to privacy an essential right, or is it harmful?

Remember, it doesn't matter what your point of view is; it's how you support it that counts. Make your case with strong examples and solid, clear reasoning.

BRAIN JAM:
Test Prep

Sharpen your words. Test day isn't the best day to start using new vocabulary words. As you practice for the verbal part of the SATs, create a running list of words that might work for an essay. Read a newspaper and circle any words you're unfamiliar with. Look them up and, if appropriate, add them to your SAT essay word list.

Take a look at the following prompts:

A powerful statement can be made without a word being spoken.

"Necessity is the mother of invention."

People can reveal a lot about themselves by the decisions or choices they make.

Decide whether you agree or disagree with each of these statements and provide one example to support your point of view.

TO FIND OUT MORE

Books

Anker, Susan. *Real Writing with Readings: Paragraphs and Essays for College, Work and Everyday Life, 3rd Edition*. New York: Bedford/St. Martin's Press, 2004.

Baygell, Ruth, ed. *Essay Writing: Step-by-Step: A Newsweek Education Program Guide for Teens*. New York: Simon and Schuster, 2003.

Bishop, Wendy. *The Subject Is Writing: Essays by Teachers and Students*. Portsmith, NH: Boyton/Cook, 2003.

Bradbury, Ray. *Zen in the Art of Writing: Essays on Creativity*. New York: Bantam, 1992.

Eggers, Dave. *The Best American Nonrequired Reading 2004*. Boston: Houghton Mifflin, 2004.

Espey, David. *Writing the Journey: Essays, Stories and Poems on Travel*. New York: Pearson Longman, 2004.

King, Stephen. *On Writing: A Memoir of the Craft*. New York: Scribner, 2000.

Sorenson, Sharon. *Webster's New World Student Writing Handbook, 4th Edition*. New York: MacMillan, 2000.

Organizations and Online Sites

Children's Express

http://www.childrens-express.org

This site contains news and comments by young authors.

Creative Writing for Teens

http://teenwriting.about.com

This site is a resource for teens on creative writing.

FLAW: The Fallout League of Adolescent Writers

http://www.angelfire.com/ct/fallout/

This site is a showplace for teen authors to post and discuss their work on the Internet.

Meryln's Pen: Fiction, Essays and Poems by America's Teens

http://www.merlynspen.org

This site gives teens information on how to get published.

Middlesex University

http://www.mdx.ac.uk/www/study/Essays1.htm#Suggestions

This site has essay topic ideas and other information on writing essays.

Skipping Stones International Multicultural Magazine

http://www.skippingstones.org

This is a publication that teens can send their work to for possible publication.

Suite 101: Young Writers

http://www.suite101.com/welcome.cfm/young_writers

This site is a complete resource for writing tips, how to get published, and a variety of other educational topics.

Teen Ink: Written by Teens Only
http://teenink.com
This site is a place for online publishing of works by teens. There are also writing tips.

TeenLit
http://www.teenlit.com
This site is a place teens can go to have their work published on the Internet. It is also an outlet for teens to discuss books and writing.

University of Birmingham: How To Write an Essay
http://www.bham.ac.uk/english/bibliography/students/essay.htm
This is a great site with additional information on writing essays.

Write an Essay
http://www.write-an-essay.com
This website gives detailed information on writing essays.

The Write Stuff
http://www.geocities.com/writestuffclub/TheWriteStuffClub.html
This site is an online writing club for writers ages thirteen to twenty-three. Teens can submit their work for peer review, get writing tips, and discuss each other's work.

Index

TAMRA ORR

I am a full-time writer living in the gorgeous Pacific Northwest. I have written more than 50 books for children and families, as well as hundreds of magazine articles and more educational-testing stories and questions than I can count. On a bad day, I look myself up on an online bookstore, and that usually cheers me up.

Coming up with ideas for books and articles is not usually a problem, since topics are assigned to me. However, all writers, including myself, have moments when their minds go blank. I usually overcome these moments by taking a break and looking at the mountains, closing my eyes and listening to music, and talking over my writer's block with my family. Other tricks I have used include scanning the indexes of reference books, leafing through new and old magazines, and reading my favorite lines from familiar books.

Writing this book was great fun for me because most of the time, I am asked to write on a topic I don't know a lot about. Those assignments taught me almost everything there is to know about doing research. Few authors can say they have written about fire ants, Ronald Reagan, test-tube babies, Lewis and Clark, terrorist groups, school violence, and Native Americans all in the same lifetime. This book, on the other hand, focused on the skills and knowledge I use every day.

I am the homeschooling mother of four children, ages nine to twenty-one, and the life partner of Joseph. I spend my six spare minutes a day reading something that has nothing to do with grammar, listening to Broadway soundtracks, talking to my husband about Volkswagens, and settling squabbles among three children with only one video game system.